Animals in Minecraft

By Josh Gregory

Published in the United States of America by
Cherry Lake Publishing
Ann Arbor, Michigan
www.cherrylakepublishing.com

Reading Adviser: Marla Conn, Read With Me Now
Photo Credits: Images by Josh Gregory

Library of Congress Cataloging-in-Publication Data has been filed and is available
at catalog.loc.gov

Cherry Lake Publishing would like to acknowledge the work of the Partnership for
21st Century Learning. Please visit *www.p21.org* for more information.

Printed in the United States of America
Corporate Graphics

Table of Contents

Cows are among the many types of animals you will come across as you play *Minecraft*.

The Amazing Animals of Minecraft

Have you ever played *Minecraft* before? There are an amazing number of things to do in its huge world. You might have noticed the many wild animals that wander around as you explore. These creatures aren't just for show. They have many uses in the world of *Minecraft*. Learning about them will make you a better player!

Chickens lay eggs, which can be used to make a variety of foods in *Minecraft*.

Working Up an Appetite

You might have noticed that your character gets hungry as you play *Minecraft*. Getting too hungry has bad effects. Your character has to eat to survive. Luckily, there is a good source of food all around. Most animals in *Minecraft* will drop meat when you attack them. Cook the meat over a fire. Then your character can enjoy a tasty meal!

If you want to find a polar bear, try climbing to the top of a tall mountain.

Creatures for Crafting

Minecraft's animals drop a lot of other useful items besides meat. Many of these items are important **crafting** ingredients. For example, sheep drop wool. You can use wool to craft string. You can use string to craft a fishing pole or a bow. Chickens drop feathers. You can use them to craft arrows for your bow!

Animals Everywhere

Different animals are found in different parts of the *Minecraft* world. You might see pigs or horses wandering in grassy areas. Polar bears are only in snowy places. Squids live underwater. Explore to find new animals!

A horse is usually the best way to get around the world in *Minecraft.*

Hitching a Ride

The world of *Minecraft* is huge. It can take a long time to reach faraway places. Animals can help you move faster! You can ride a horse to run quicker and jump higher. Believe it or not, you can also ride a pig.

Animals can help you carry things, too. Donkeys and mules can carry chests. You can store anything you want in these chests.

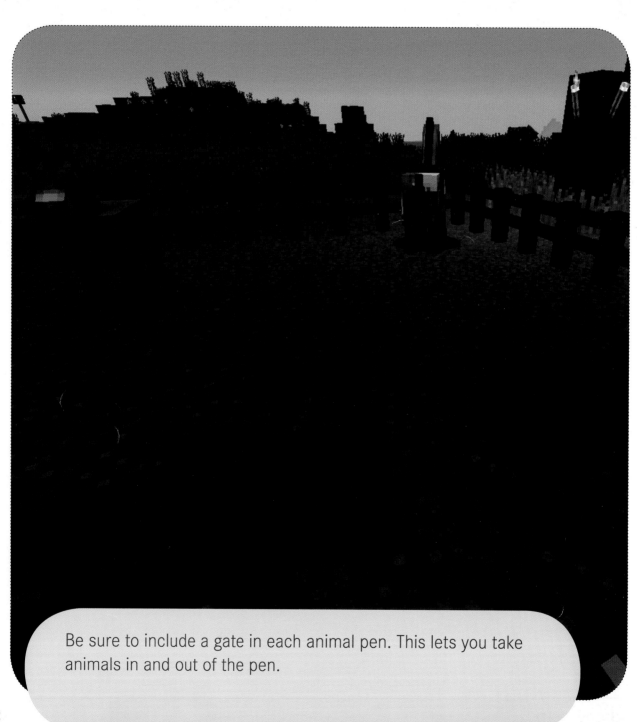

Be sure to include a gate in each animal pen. This lets you take animals in and out of the pen.

Building a Farm

You'll need a farm if you want to start collecting animals in *Minecraft*. Build a farmhouse for yourself. Then start making pens for your animals. You can craft fence pieces from wooden **planks** and sticks. Build a few large, fenced-in areas. You'll need one pen for each type of animal you want on your farm.

Pigs love carrots! If you hold one, every nearby pig will follow you everywhere you go.

Making Friends with Wildlife

Now you need animals to put in your pens. You can see the animals wandering around. But how can you get them to your farm? Each type of animal has a favorite food. Hold that food in your hand, and the animal will follow you. Now you can lead the animal back to your farm!

Favorite Foods

Here are some examples of animals' favorite foods.
Pig: carrot, potato, or beet
Sheep: wheat
Cow: wheat
Chicken: seeds

Press the Use button on a pet dog to make it sit. Press the button again to tell the animal to stand and start following you again.

From Wild to Tame

Some animals need to be **tamed** before you can use them. Try to ride a wild horse or donkey. It will throw you off its back! Keep trying until the horse or donkey lets you ride it. Now it is tame! It will not throw you off its back. But you need to use a saddle if you want to control the animal's direction. You can also tame wild wolves and **ocelots**. If you feed a wild dog bones, it might turn into a tame pet dog. Feeding a wild ocelot fish can turn it into a pet cat.

You can give your character and horse matching armor. This will help keep both of them safe in battle.

Protecting Your Animals

You can ride your horse into battle against enemy **mobs**. Try giving it **armor** to protect it from attacks. Your pet dog will also follow you and help fight enemies. If your horse or dog gets hit, it will lose health. Feed your animal to heal it. Dogs eat meat. Horses like apples, carrots, hay, and wheat.

Horse, Donkey, or Mule?

Horses, donkeys, and mules look a lot alike in *Minecraft*. You can ride all three. But each one is very different. Horses are the fastest, but they cannot carry chests. Horses are also the only animals that can wear armor.

Try building a huge farm with all kinds of animals. Then you will always have all the animal supplies you need for your adventures!

What's Next?

There are a lot of other cool things you can do with animals in *Minecraft*. Did you know you can **dye** your sheep different colors? You can also change the color of your dog's collar. Do you want more animals on your farm? Try **breeding** your animals. You can have a whole farm full of baby pigs, horses, and more. Experiment and be creative as you play. You never know what you'll discover!

Glossary

armor (AR-mur) protective clothing your character can wear in *Minecraft*

breeding (BREED-ing) allowing animals to mate and produce offspring

crafting (KRAFT-ing) making or creating

dye (DYE) to change the color of something

mobs (MAHBZ) in *Minecraft*, any living, moving beings within the game

ocelots (AH-suh-lahts) a type of wildcat with spotted fur

planks (PLANGKS) long, flat pieces of wood

tamed (TAYMD) trained to live with or be useful to people

Find Out More

Books

Jelley, Craig. *Minecraft: Guide to Creative*. New York: Del Rey, 2017.

Milton, Stephanie. *Minecraft Essential Handbook*. New York: Scholastic, 2015.

Web Sites

Minecraft

https://minecraft.net/en
At the official *Minecraft* Web site, you can learn more about the game or download a copy of the PC version.

Minecraft Wiki

https://minecraft.gamepedia.com/Minecraft_Wiki
Minecraft's many fans work together to maintain this detailed guide to the game.

Index

About the Author

Josh Gregory is the author of more than 125 books for kids. He has written about everything from animals to technology to history. A graduate of the University of Missouri–Columbia, he currently lives in Chicago, Illinois.